Whisperings of the Spirit

Marcie McNutt

AuthorHouse™
1663 Liberty Drive
Bloomington, IN 47403
www.authorhouse.com
Phone: 1-800-839-8640

First published by AuthorHouse 10/5/2010

ISBN: 978-1-4520-7028-5 (e)
ISBN: 978-1-4520-7027-8 (sc)

Library of Congress Control Number: 2010912811

Printed in the United States of America

This book is printed on acid-free paper.

In Memory

In memory of my saintly father Albert G. Jacobs whose gentle, loving ways and prayerful life were an inspiration to me and to all who had the privilege of knowing him

In Gratitude

In gratitude to my dear husband Don, for the many hours he has devoted to helping ready this work for publication, and to our youngest daughter, Sheri Mahoney, for the tremendous blessing she has been to us during this time sharing her computer knowledge. A special thanks also to my caring sister, Lou Rademacher, for her much needed guidance, encouragement and availability. In particular, my deep gratitude to the Holy Spirit for inspiring these poems for without His impartation this book would not be in print.

The Rose

The rose reminds me of Jesus
Who is ever so special to me
For many the rose is most favored
Of all the flowers you see

Its gentle fragrance is lovely
And brings comfort to the one who receives
So also the word Jesus preached to men
Especially to all who believed

Jesus presence commanded attention
The beauty of the rose does the same
It's the flower that represents lovers
Jesus also can make that claim

The message He spoke was often of love
Of sharing and caring and giving
Roses also speak of all these things
Such a lovely touch for the living

Roses and thorns go together
It was thorns Jesus wore on His head
He willingly died, was crucified
His blood for all humans was shed

The life of the rose brings happiness
Before is comes to its end
But our lives with Christ after death will go on
How splendid is that my friend?

The One Who's From Above

My heart is full of gratefulness
For the One who died for me
Because of His great sacrifice
I'm no more bound but free

He fills me up with so much love
He's gifted me with peace
The more love I give back to Him
The more He gives increase

He's generous with His blessings
And freely grants His grace
I've come to love our meetings
In the quiet secret place

Now my heart belongs to Him
His guidance to obey
Whatever plan He has for me
I'll do without delay

And with zeal and dedication
I'll follow through with love
Giving all I've got for Him
The One who's from above

God's Gifts Are A Treasure

Blessed Redeemer
You were sent from above
To bring to Gods' creatures
His infinite love

God's gifts are a treasure
We depend on each day
To strengthen and help us
As we walk in His way

Daily He beckons
And it's when we comply
That He's able to touch us
From His home in the sky

He's so eager to help us
And wants us to know
It makes His heart happy
When we blossom and grow

What a blessing it is
When we open our hearts
And welcome our Savior
For that's where it all starts

A Sonnet

Oh mighty God in Heaven
I come before You now
To worship and to praise You
And in adoration bow

You bless me with Your presence
As I draw close to You
And in the frequent storms of life
You're the One who sees me through

You amaze me with the answers
To the many prayers I bring
My heart wells up with gratefulness
Which makes me want to sing

And as I seek Your precious face
My hunger grows and grows
And deep within my heart I want
A sonnet to compose

To let You know how wonderful
You are to me each day
These are the pure intentions
I so desire to convey

Gems Of Great Worth

Peace belongs-to God's people whose songs
Delight our Father on high
He loves to behold-both young and old
Serenading Him up in the sky

It warms each part-of His tender heart
For on all who set Him aglow
He smiles from above and sends down His love
On these choicest blessings will flow

He takes pleasure when they-seek to obey
His word written down in the past
Our Father is blest-when His own do their best
For that's when their progress will last

Day after day-they are seen as they pray
By the One looking down upon earth
Rewards they shall reap and He blesses their sleep
In His eyes they are gems of great worth

I'll Rely On Your Promise

I come to You Lord in a spirit of reverence
Seeking to know You more intimately
Open my mind to receive revelation
And my heart to worship Your majesty

My aim is to please You whatever the cost
And to reflect Your dear likeness each day
Lovingly grant me Your special graces
So I'm faithful to follow Your way

For the road that I travel often gets rocky
The troubles of life crowd in like a snare
Strengthen my trust in Your presence among us
I'll rely on Your promise to always be there

The Ultimate Cure

What a beautiful Savior You are
You're more radiant than any star
You're holy and pure, the ultimate cure
All that is precious You are

What a blessing to call on Your Name
You Lord are always the same
Faithful and true, how we dearly love You
Heaven with You is our aim

When You take us to be with You there
We'll be ever under Your care
Safe in Your arms, away from all harm
Sweet praises to You - we'll declare

Called To Obey

Your blessings overtake
The ones who forsake
All else to follow You
We are called to obey
Without delay
Which all who love You will do

Your Word spells it out
Without any doubt
We must love all our enemies
Lord this we will do
In obedience to You
For our Savior we so long to please

So extend Your dear graces
In all the right places
And help us always to choose
The best path to take
Right choices we'll make
Your blessings we don't want to lose

It Is Jesus

I race to that place
Where I come face to face
With the One Who gives grace
It is Jesus

It's there I can feel
Far beyond what is real
In the quiet I kneel
Before Jesus

I'm speaking of He
Who's so loving to me
I'm sure you can see
It is Jesus

He's above all the rest
Far surpasses the test
He's my favorite guest
That's my Jesus

The Blessed Printed Page

Spiritual food is what we need
To feed our hungry souls
And it comes from the precious word of God
Not from our cereal bowls

We need every word from the Bible
To nourish and sustain
It's wonderful lessons and teachings
Will be for us great gain

For none of God's dear children
Can get out of the babyhood stage
Without a daily soaking in
Of the blessed printed page

So we'll not let our Bibles get dusty
Nor bury them in a drawer
We will feed and be strong and full of God's word
Then when the enemy comes near to roar

We will surely defeat him in battle
Cause God's word is what makes us wise
And however the foe may appear to us
We'll not be fooled by his disguise

That Place Up Above

I love my King my Savior and Lord
And never tire of telling You so
My heart longs to be, ever closer to Thee
And warmed by Your radiant glow

How exciting dear Lord to dream of Your Kingdom
There'll be singing and merriment there
Surrounded by love, in that place up above
What a glorious atmosphere

Peace, contentment and love will prevail
In that place that's waiting for me
I don't want to miss, the never-ending bliss
That will continue eternally

Each day draws me nearer to the time of Your coming
When joy will abound in my soul
I'm patiently waiting, my heart escalating
For it's then I'll be truly made whole

None Escape His Gaze

Each moment spent in praising God
Is fruitful in every way
It blesses Him and gives us joy
How better to start each day

It warms God's heart and makes Him glad
He sent His precious Son
To bring His loving message
To each and everyone

It's important then to keep in mind
And be faithful in it too
That what we give we reap in kind
When judgment day is due

Some take heed and some do not
But none escape His gaze
Rich blessings fall upon the ones
Who heed His loving ways

For All That He Provides

From heaven our caring Father
Watches over us from above
Guiding us by His wisdom
And teaching us how to love

He surrounds us daily with angels
And gifts us with caring friends
He places His beauty around us
His goodness never ends

He's the Creator of the universe
And every thing in it you see
From the highest lofty mountain
To the tiniest honey bee

So each new day when we awake
And open wide our eyes
Let's send up loving thanks to Him
For all that He provides

Golden Nuggets

Your Word to me is pure gold
It is truth it is wholesome and clean
It teaches me how to live for You Lord
From it golden nuggets I glean

If my Bible were taken from me
It would seem like a part of me died
The precious infilling of Your holy Word
Keeps me daily satisfied

Please deepen my hunger for more
For Your message is just what I need
If I'm to be a vessel for You
On the truth of Your Word I must feed

As I grow in the knowledge of You
I'll be prepared for what lies ahead
My faith's growing stronger day after day
Thank You Lord for my daily bread

When My Life Is Through

Early every morning
I come to You to pray
That You'll fill me with Your goodness
And Your Spirit has full sway

I need Your graces daily Lord
So I can live for You
And share Your love with others
The way You want me to

Please give me Your instruction
Guide me where to go
Whatever good may come from it
All to You dear Lord I'll owe

So fill me now with all I need
I give my life to You
And I'll rejoice for all You've done
When my life is through

Lasting Joy

The God we love is awesome
His ways surpass our own
His plans we cannot fathom
We place our trust in Him alone

We know He never makes mistakes
So we can trust His choice
If we listen in the stillness
We can clearly hear His voice

We need His guidance daily
Lest we should slip away
For if we choose another route
From His wise path we'll stray

It's best to daily follow Him
Wherever He may lead
And minister to others
When we sense there is a need

What follows is a lasting joy
God chooses to impart
Not only deep down in the soul
But also in the heart

My Sincerest Goal

To sing Your praises oh my God
With all my heart and soul
Through all the moments that You give
Is my sincerest goal

And whether they be rough or smooth
Is not the issue here
I long to go on praising You
Each day throughout each year

There may be days of darkness Lord
When I cannot see Your face
But I'll praise You and I'll trust You
And be guided by Your grace

For each new day that I awake
Is a blessing from Your hand
And without Your grace extended Lord
I could not rise or stand

Nor could I think or reason
Or make a single sound
Oh then I could not praise You Lord
And feel my joy abound

Oh Lord I ever thank You
For life for breath and voice
For with these gifts You've given
I can with You rejoice

Oh Lord as long as I have breath
I'll lift my hands to Thee
And praise Your Name forevermore
With love to You from me

He's With Me

Oh what a blessed joy it is
To house the Savior of my soul
Within this earthen vessel
As I take my daily stroll

He's with me during morning chores
And when the day's half done
He walks with me throughout the day
Till the setting of the sun

However many things I do
Throughout my busy day
I have the Savior of the world
Walking with me all the way

And when I settle down to sleep
He's with me even then
To hold me tight throughout the night
I praise You Lord, Amen

When All The Work Is Through

Jesus look into my heart
And tell me what You see
Any ugliness that's there
Please point it out to me

As much as I may want to change
I can't do it on my own
But need Your help and guidance
If the truth is to be known

Please help me Lord to listen
To what You have to say
And I'll sense Your Spirit move in me
As I begin to pray

I'll do my best to trust You
To complete what I can't do
And then we'll see a miracle
When all the work is through

My heart will fill so full of praise
Your joy will overflow
And somewhere in the process
I'll take on Your gentle glow

And when I do I'll let it shine
On everyone I meet
And as that light draws them to You
They'll not be incomplete

A Place Of Pure Refreshment

I love the secret chamber Lord
I love the secret place
It's there I find contentment
And Your warmth upon my face

What a place of pure refreshment
Where You give Yourself to me
It's there I gain a full supply
And have more to give back to Thee

It's my favorite place to linger Lord
For Your joy begins to flow
It refreshes like a waterfall
And soon begins to grow

Into a bubbling fountain
That makes me want to sing
Praises to my Savior
My Rock - my Friend - my King

The Tapestry

Our lives are like a tapestry
I believe this to be true
God has a plan for each of us
His plan we should pursue

The trials that we encounter
Throughout our days on earth
Make up the threads He uses
To weave a tapestry of worth

But that can only happen
In the many trials we face
When we react as Jesus would
Sometimes that's not the case

So when we fail we try again
And with God's grace extended
We will make steady progress
When we see our failures ended

Left on our own we flounder
But if we call on Him to lead
Our days will run much smoother
We may even gain some speed

God will help us reach our goal
And when the tapestry is done
The Kingdom doors will open wide
For life's battles will be won

Imagine

Imagine if each one of us
Would take the time to be
Daily in the presence of
The Man from Galilee

It could just be the turning point
For a world that's gone astray
If we'd rid ourselves of needless things
And knuckle down to pray

Our focus ought to be on Him
Who died to set us free
For all He did while here on earth
Was done for you and me

And all because He loved us so
Beyond our comprehension
If only we could grasp this thought
Maybe then we'd pay attention

And speedily get at the task
Of carrying out His plan
To bring His loving message
To every hungry man

He Changes Each Heart

High up above lives the God that we love
Yet He lives in our hearts as well
As He fills us inside-and within doth abide
He brings changes I love to retell

First He changes each heart and sets it apart
For He sees the value of each
Then He works His wonders-He never blunders
All He has He puts within reach

He changes our minds whenever He finds
That which He knows is not best
For the child of His love-who's been born from above
He supplies the most wonderful rest

He calls this His peace we can have without cease
If we follow the rules He sets down
The choice is our own-but He will not condone
If upon His laws we do frown

When we get ourselves still and conform to His will
It brings a smile to His face
Then He's free to bless-and loves to caress
Every child who seeks His embrace

The Finger Of God

A few feet from my window
Stands a strong and sturdy pine
And on a branch a feeder hangs
Where the songbirds come to dine

It gives me great enjoyment
To watch them feast and linger
I marvel as I contemplate
Their creation by God's finger

All around I see God's handiwork
His stamp upon all things
The seas, the bees, the lovely trees
To my soul a song it brings

His splendor is seen in the sky each day
And throughout the countryside
All that my eyes can ever behold
The Creator beautified

My heart wells up with thanks to Him
His awesomeness I'll praise
I'll bless His Name for that's my aim
In my remaining days

My Destination

Today I got to thinking
What can I bring to Jesus?
Besides the love I give Him every day
And as I pondered deeper
My mind became enlightened
To be kind to all in what I do and say

For what I do to others
It is written in the scriptures
I also do to Jesus whom I love
And if I'm reading it correctly
Then I'd better be determined
For He oversees it all from up above

As I seek to enter deeper
In my relationship with Jesus
I know He will direct me on my way
As I follow in His footsteps
I'll reach my destination
If I listen to His voice and then obey

Because Of Calvary

There's no one in this universe
You do not wish to touch
With Your healing and forgiveness
For You love each one so much

Your love is vast and awesome
It encompasses the earth
Each life is precious to You Lord
None can estimate its worth

Your eye is ever searching for
That one who's lost his way
Your ever-loving faithful heart
Wants to bring him home to stay

You paid the price so long ago
When you hung upon the tree
And opened Heaven wide for all
Because of Calvary

His Fingerprints

Every day I marvel
At God's handiwork on earth
His fingerprints are everywhere
Revealing things of worth

He out does Himself in nature
Whatever scene He may unfold
Comes directly from His palate
As a masterpiece of old

I love to drink God's beauty in
It warms my heart and soul
And strengthens life within me
I'm sure this must have been His goal

For He is wise, does all things well
And never ever blunders
I'll thank Him reverently each day
For His majestic wonders

The Death Of Self

I come before You Jesus
With a big request for You
And when You've thought it over
Please send Your answer through

You call us all to serve You
We can do that best when we
Are emptied out of all that's us
Then filled up full with Thee

Bring about the death of self
In me my blessed Savior
I give myself to You to use
Please alter my behavior

Change everything You see in me
That does not please You Lord
I evermore desire to be
With You in one accord

And once dear Lord I'm emptied out
Then into me please pour
The gifts You see I'm lacking
And I'll serve You evermore

A Blessed Treasure Without Measure

Precious Jesus, precious Jesus
How I long to sing Your praises
How I long to bow before You
And to tenderly adore You

Inside my heart is a constant longing
To worship You as the angels do
Never ceasing-praise increasing
Till its fervency delights You

You placed this longing deep within me
Dearest Savior-dearest King
A blessed treasure without measure
For which my soul doth sing

I give to You a willing heart
A yielded heart for You to fill
And my simple childlike plea
To always do Your perfect will

Send Your Spirit fresh upon me
And in a mighty move of power
Sweep away all interference
That I might please You every hour

Lantern In The Window

Above the swirling waters
Of the storms of life I'll rest
Safe in the arms of my Savior
For to me He gives His best

To all who trust in Him-He's true
For it delights His heart
When we cast all our cares on Him
And let Him play His part

Our Heavenly Father wants to be
So close to every child
May those of His who've strayed away
To Him be reconciled

His love is such it knows no bounds
And it is freely shared
With every creature on this earth
Who wants his life repaired

With tenderness He patiently waits
For our return to Him
His lanterns in the window
And it's light is never dim

Walking In His Will

We read God's word and that is good
But then when we are through
Let's take it one step further
For what His word says we must do

Instead of living our way
And wasting precious time
If we follow His instructions
In our spirit lives we'll climb

God's words are filled with wisdom
To guide us in His ways
As we absorb His messages
He will direct our days

And we'll be so much happier
When closely walking in His will
Knowing God is pleased with us
As His desires we fulfill

I Want The World To Know

How I love You Jesus
You are everything to me
For me You bled and suffered
And died upon a tree

How I long to serve You
And do it blissfully
Until You come to take me home
For all eternity

Wrap Your arms around me
And never let me go
You cleansed me with Your blood Lord
And washed me white as snow

You fill me with Your joy Lord
And set my heart aglow
And all that You have done for me
I want the world to know

Beacon Lights

Let me be Your beacon light
Shining brightly day and night
Beckoning the lost to You
So that You can make them new

For their empty lives seen vain
Most of them are feeling pain
They are searching high and low
But for what they do not know

I know Jesus what they need
It's on You dear Lord they need to feed
And when they find what their searching for
They'll be hungry for so much more

Then when they're filled
So full of You
You'll send them out
To be beacons too

Rare Beauty

Each day when I awake dear God
There's much to thank You for
A brand-new start, joy in my heart
Old friends and so much more

The blessing of my family
So caring warm and true
From the love they share, I am aware
Their source dear God is You

My eyesight is a blessing Lord
With which I can behold
A rainbow high, up in the sky
Streaked with purple, green and gold

The songs of the birds You send my way
As they come to bathe and feed
Lovely flowers, I can view for hours
Springing up from a tiny seed

The sight of a spider spinning its web
Or a butterfly in flight
Each of these things, what joy it brings
To my heart prompting waves of delight

You Lord are the Creator of all these gifts
And You in Your all-wise design
Decided to bless us and also caress us
With rare beauty that can't be defined

The Keeper Of The Sheep

Tis' so sweet dear Lord to sit at Your feet
In the stillness of the night
And partake of the rays of Your gentle gaze
And be warmed by Your heavenly light

A gift so rare is the love that we share
While the world is fast asleep
In my thoughts I'm alone sitting by the throne
With the Keeper of the sheep

This to me is a treasure worth much more than gold
Or diamonds or pearls and such
But a treasure to cherish that can never perish
A blessing-a God given touch

You impart to me the warmth of Your love
And cradle me in Your peace
I picture Your face-feel immersed in Your grace
And instantly feel sweet release

Now I know what You give I must share
I'm most willing to do as You say
Let flow out of me whatever You see
Will bless others You lead down my way

Time Is Fleeting

Remember time is fleeting
Much has already gone
How much remains we do not know
We may not see another dawn

Each moment is a gift from God
And to be loved and treasured
So we must always be on guard
Our days have all been measured

Those that remain we must not waste
But spend in reaching out
To bless all those we hold most dear
That's what our lives are all about

For we cannot give God's love away
Without it soon returning
To flood our souls with endless joy
And make us more discerning

Jesus Is My Hero

Jesus is my hero
For Him I want to shine
At the marriage supper
It's Him with Whom I'll dine

I belong to Jesus
And He is ever mine
The day I enter Heavens gates
Our hearts will intertwine

I am ever grateful
To Him who saved my soul
Jesus is my treasure
And Heaven is my goal

Blessings fall upon us
As we His Name extol
Thankful I will ever be
To the One Who makes me whole

Your Perfect Will

The sweetest thing to do
Is to fellowship with You
And as You share with me
New wonders do I see

You open wide my heart
Your treasures to impart
I welcome them inside
Where Your Spirit doth abide

As I receive from You
And gain a clearer view
You send me out dear Lord
With You in one accord

Please set my heart aflame
I want to glorify Your Name
By living to fulfill
Your plan, Your perfect will

For You I'll Gladly Live

Lord I cannot make it on my own
I give You all my cares
And place them in Your loving arms
Along with all my prayers

Nor can I see with blurry eyes
Please take my heartaches too
In their place give me Your peace
In all I say and do

I thank you Lord for hearing me
And granting this exchange
For what You've done is awesome
This blessing You've arranged

What a joy to feel Your peace
A special gift from Thee
Enveloping my total self
And liberating me

Please fill me once again oh Lord
With all You have to give
And with Your love and grace in me
For You I'll gladly live

God's Lighthouse

What if the desire I have in my heart
Is from God and in need of attention
What if He wants me to get quiet with Him
And seek His divine intervention

Sometimes He puts rich things on our hearts
That we ought not let slip away
Wonderful treasures to share with others
And to them be a sweet bouquet

I'd like to be God's lighthouse on earth
To reflect what He pours in my heart
Ever giving His treasures away
Grateful as those blessings depart

Foe whatever we give away in His Name
If given with a heart full of love
Will return to bless the giver
And delight our God up above

King Of Kings

Oh Lord we lift our voices
In gratefulness to You
We sing out praises to Your Name
With hearts sincere and true

Your love was such You gave Your Son
To die and rise again
To set us free from all our sins
And vindicate all men

With gladness Lord we will rejoice
In all we say and do
And in so doing hope to bring
Much glory unto You

Whatever time we may have left
However long that be
We want to magnify Your Name
And give honor unto Thee

For You are worthy dearest Lord
Of all our adoration
One day we'll crown You King of kings
And enjoy Your coronation

Speak To Us Lord And Help Us To Hear You

As we come to You Lord in a spirit of reverence
Seeking to know You in a more intimate way
Open our minds to receive revelation
And open our hearts as to how we should pray

For our aim is to please You the God that we serve
And to move on in the spiritual path that we trod
Speak to us Lord and help us to hear You
So that we may avoid the correction rod

We know in Your wisdom You see so much more
Than the insight that's given to us
Do as You please, have Your way with us Lord
Even though we should but up a fuss

For Your ways are eternal and high above ours
And we know that You make no mistake
Whatever the trials You bring good from them Lord
And all this You do for our sake

Tho sometimes we question the things that befall us
We know in the end it's been good
For the lessons we learn in the battles of life
Draw us closer to You as they should

God Is Never Late

Jesus Christ my Savior
Has become my closest friend
I know He's always with me
And will be to the end

I can count on Him to help me
When I find myself in need
He's always ever ready
I don't even have to plead

But there are times I recognize
The blessing that He sends
Comes in a form I really think
He wouldn't give His friends

Yet down the road I do perceive
He had the best in mind
When He in His great wisdom
Sent a blessing of that kind

He loves it when we trust in Him
For He knows all we lack
It's up to us to quiet down
Then He'll pick up the slack

And tho it's tough to wait on Him
The benefits are great
For He'll work out every detail
And God is never late

I'll Follow Where He Leads

My heart is full of gratefulness
To The One Who died for me
Because of His great sacrifice
I'm no more bound but free

He fills my heart with so much love
He gifts me with His peace
And the more love I return to Him
The more He gives increase

He's generous with His blessings
And freely shares His grace
I've come to love our meetings
In the quiet secret place

Now my life belongs to Him
The One who meets my needs
With zeal and dedication
I'll follow where He leads

A New Dimension

Oh glorious God to worship You
Is the reason we've been created
What a wonderful privilege and also a joy
And a reason to get excited

We don't praise You to put on a show
We don't do it to get attention
As we honor and worship the Lord we love
We then enter a new dimension

Our hearts ascend to a higher realm
In this spiritual enterprise
We move up and on to a new plateau
Where there is no compromise

We give our best to our Savior and King
And before Him His grace we implore
And as we do His blessings come down
Even more than ever before

The Names And Titles Of God

You are The Bright and Morning Star
What a wonder oh God You are
You are The Keeper of each soul
Guarding Your dear ones is truly Your goal

Known as Wonderful Councilor
Our minds surely need an open door
And what a Shepherd You are to the sheep
Over Your flock You tenderly weep

You are The Way The Truth and The Life
Following You puts an end to strife
Jesus You're The Light of the world to us all
Enlighten our minds so we do not fall

Also known as The Gate are You
Not many get in but only a few
The Deliverer is another name we know
Setting men free from the ugly foe

You're also called The Conquering One
By Your death on the cross the victory's been won
Your Names and Titles are many we know
By learning each one we shall surely grow

Gods Handiwork

The God of this great universe
Is not hard to get to know
One can clearly picture Him
In the delicate flakes of snow

In the stars that shine so bright as night
Or a rainbow after the rain
In a gentle breeze caressing the trees
In a hymn with a haunting refrain

God's handiwork is everywhere
Revealing His love for all
Spilling over the whole wide world
Like a glorious waterfall

He poured His beauty over the earth
To display His caring heart
Welcoming all who are listening
To draw near and become a part

How to respond to this generous God
It is up to us to decide
Hopefully with a resounding yes
For in us He wants to abide

The One Who Beckoned

It's so very very quiet Lord
So peaceful all around
And though I'm really straining Lord
I can barely hear a sound

I'm listening for Your footsteps
Cause I long to be with You
The precious times we have to share
Seem all too few

But I'm not complaining Jesus
For I love every single second
And I know it's all been pre-arranged
Because You're the One who beckoned

And I'm so thrilled You did Lord
Because it's oh so very true
That every time we fellowship
I feel closer Lord to You

Pour Your Contents Deep Within Us

What an awesome God you are Lord
Your ways are far above our own
Your plans for us we cannot fathom
We place our trust in You alone

Teach us dear Lord to be led by Your Spirit
For this we truly need to know
Make us to be a yielded people
For it's then Your body can truly grow

You choose to live within Your people
That the world might see Your light in them
Please send Your Spirit fresh upon us
And keep that light from growing dim

Please purify these temples Jesus
Disinfect them through and through
Remove each trace of all that clogs them
So all that can be seen is You

Heart of Jesus ever faithful
Overflowing with love divine
Pour Your contents deep within us
So through each vessel You might shine

Your Gentle Ways

You are my rock and my refuge
And my strength at times I feel weak
Whenever a storm is raging
It's Your arms of love I seek

It's a blessing to know You are near Lord
Responding when I call Your Name
Your gentle ways draw me close to You
And set my heart aflame

No place on earth can ever compare
To that one where Your presence reigns
Blessed are all who dwell therein
In them Your peace ever remains

I Welcome Your Nearness

Your precious love is a gift from above
Bringing comfort to my soul
I feel a sweet calm like a soothing balm
Lord it's You my heart longs to extol

Each moment is sweet sitting by Your feet
Where I'm free to commune with You
I welcome Your nearness and soak in Your dearness
All else disappears from view

How it saddens me when it's time to flee
From that peaceful place I treasure
The pleasantness there is beyond compare
A gift I love beyond measure

New Life

I'm in need of You Lord and I can't get enough
Of the riches You give away
There's an ever-increasing thirst in me
Please fill it oh Lord I pray

For no child of Yours who's depleted and empty
Can ever hope to give out
Unless he first receives from You
Something worth shouting about

So fill me up with a brand new supply
Of that which You want me to share
I'll praise and thank You and give You the glory
For how You did answer my prayer

Lives will be touched, lives will be changed
And all because of Your giving
Hallelujah and praise to Your Name
For You give new life to the living

Sweet Sleep

Sweet sleep is a blessing You freely give
To all who surrender to You
Happy are they in Your service Lord
Who do what You call them to

Daily serving the Savior well
Asking for naught in return
Blest are they and full of Your joy
And grateful for all that they learn

Eager are they to share with others
The wisdom You've given to them
Knowing their "yes" is dear to Your heart
Your approval of them is a gem

At nightfall they sleep most peacefully
Aware the day was well spent
Before drifting off they see Your sweet smile
Confident their Lord is content

Our Prayer Line Telephone

God's ways are so much wiser
Than we mortals will ever know
If we would learn to lean on Him
In patience we would grow

It really does not make much sense
To tackle problems on our own
When we can get such great results
On our "prayer line telephone"

It only takes a moment
To reach our heavenly Father's place
His throne room door is always open
And He's happy to take our case

We've brought many requests before Him
Time and time again
He answers each in His perfect will
And He's good at it, Amen!

However God chooses to work things out
We can surely trust His ways
His solution will be the perfect one
Even if there are delays

Gods' Perfect Design

Our God has a place for us all
We ought always to be open to His gentle call
For if we get in line-with His perfect design
We'll be at peace what're might befall

He is our guide from above
His guidance comes straight from His love
We may not now know, where He wants us to go
But He'll prod us with the ease of a dove

Our Father never makes mistakes
He will gently put on the brakes
If we get caught up with man and get out of His plan
We'll be breaking the laws that He makes

As we wait on our dear Lord in prayer
We will surely be aware that He's there
Bringing forth the advice, that will surely suffice
And relief from the burdens we bear

We need to take heed to God's voice
And in Him to daily rejoice
If we choose to obey, in our walk day by day
We'll have peace that we made the right choice

Fervent Prayers

Good morning blessed Savior
We reverence You so much
On those for whom you'd have us pray
We ask a special touch

We so respect your awesomeness
And call on You this hour
Trusting in You to beckon the lost
By Your great and mighty power

For nothing is impossible
With the God of all creation
For You are able to bring unto Yourself
A whole entire nation

So we continue our fervent prayers
As You have inspired us to
And we are expecting miracles
Before our God is through

What a tremendous joy it is
To work with our Lord up above
Aware many souls will surrender their lives
To the King of all kings Who is love

High Above The Call Of The World

Lord I know there is so much more
In the Spirit realm for me
Much much more than I've known before
And I seek it earnestly

Lift me high above the call of the world
To a place where I'm all alone
With the One I adore where there's so much more
Than I've ever previously known

For I desire to partake
Of all You have to give
I come to You sincere and true
Please teach me how to live

In such a way You are glorified
And Your Name is lifted on high
Let Your life in me shine radiantly
As self is crucified

Please hear my cry for more of You
Shining through my being
To touch a lost and dying world
That You and I are seeing

There is such a burden on my heart
For souls to come to You
Please melt away every trace of decay
So each soul can be born anew

He Took My Place

I sing my songs unto the Lord
And let my praises rise
Until they reach God's heavenly throne
And come before His eyes

Oh how I want to bless my King
Who bled and died for me
He took my place on Calvary's cross
And has truly set me free

He took my sins upon Himself
Bore all my guilt and shame
And as He did that awesome deed
He made me whole again

Oh what a blessed Savior
Oh what a precious Lord
He alone is worthy
To be evermore adored

The Source

There is peace and refreshment in You Lord
You are a haven for all who need rest
As you welcome us into Your presence
You bless us with all that is best

You ease our pain and our suffering
As we let go of the burdens we bear
To bask in Your nearness dear Jesus
For we know that Your Spirit is there

You are the Source of all comfort
You are near to refresh and console
Till we reach Your heavenly Kingdom
Which in the end is our goal

In His Footsteps

Sweet Lamb of God how I long to trod
In Your footsteps along life's way
Though the climb will be steep I know You will keep
Your little one close day by day

So that I do not stumble and begin to grumble
And sadly begin to stray
I know there'll be pain but also great gain
For the committed do not betray

I will follow my Master but never move faster
Even though He should delay
His grace shall sustain me let nothing detain me
Whatever the price I will pay

He's Number One

The Lord our God who makes us all
Is number one with me
As I share with you some reasons why
I'm sure you will agree

He's the One you've read about
Who multiplied the loaves
And performed His many wonders
Which brought people out in droves

They came to see and hear Him
And clung to every word
Then passed along to others
The message that they heard

With love He raised the dead to life
He caused the blind to see
Jesus healed the sick and blest them
And He set the captives free

Amazing are the things He does
Even in our day
Who else produces miracles
When folks intently pray

He cares for us and meets our needs
He gives a listening ear
And to all who call upon His Name
He sends His angels near

That Very Special Moment

One day the loving God we serve
Who seems so far away
Will say our time on earth is up
And call us home to stay

It will surely be a blessing
For those who love Him so
To enter Heavens pearly gates
And leave life's cares below

I'm sure we'll all be quite amazed
At what we see up there
We'll have to stop and catch our breath
For Heavens beauty will be rare

God's paradise is full of light
Beyond our comprehension
Lovely angels everywhere
Gaining our attention

We'll see our family members
And friends from long ago
Thoughts of what awaits us there
Set my heart aglow

But that very special moment
I look forward to the most
Is when I see my Saviors face?
My Lord, my God, my Host

Thank You Dear God

Thank You dear God for this brand new day
And for all the blessings You send my way
For they are many and varied it's true
And each one of them can be traced back to You

Thank You Lord for family and friends
To each one of them Your love extends
They are all under Your watchful eye
And when they are hurting You hear their cry

I thank You dear God for the beauty of fall
And for the dearness of memories I love to recall
For sunshine and snowflakes and smiles that delight
And for stars that do twinkle and shine in the night

For beautiful gardens and children at play
Spectacular sunsets as night follows day
Peaceable landscapes with horses grazing
Picnics at campsites with bonfires blazing

And I'm so grateful for the song of the birds
And letters that arrive full of loving words
Phone calls that come that encourage my heart
And add to my memories I pray won't depart

Thank You dear God for my eyesight and hearing
And for all I behold that is most endearing
Thank you for grandkids and the love that they bring
Thank You dear God for everything

My Heavenly Guide

I plunge myself into Your heart
To hide away with Thee
And as I do Your soothing love
Gently washes over me

Caressing me and healing me
Of the wounds You see inside
I trust You Lord to do what's best
For You are my Heavenly Guide

In the quiet moments I spend with You
Help me to clearly hear
I don't want to miss a word You say
Whisper softly into my ear

I open my heart to all You desire
My life I surrender to You
Bring forth the changes needed in me
I'll be usable when You are through

All That Is Blessed Comes From Your Hand

Lord You are filled with all that we long for
All that is blessed comes from Your hand
Open our hearts and pour in what is lacking
So we can share it with those in our dying land

Bring about healing to the wounds deep within us
Change everything in us that needs to be changed
Make us shine like the Son of the Father who formed us
For from the beginning it was all pre-arranged

We trust You to do it for Your will shall be done
We've all been created in the image of Your Son
Make haste Heavenly Father and bring this about
Our hearts shall be cleansed all that taints routed out

We will fully surrender to all that You choose
For we know in our hearts we have nothing to lose
But our pride and our selfishness indifference and greed
These we are eager to lose we can't wait to be freed

So the work that You've chosen for us to get done
Can be quickly accomplished and then we shall run
Into the arms of our Savior whom we love and adore
To spend life everlasting praising Him evermore

My Dearest Friend

No relationship down here on earth
Could ever please me more
Than the one I have with Jesus
And I know there's more in store

For when this present life is over
Our relationship won't end
But it will only be enriched
For He's my dearest friend

I know he'll love me tenderly
And I'll return the same
His peace and joy will flood my soul
And set my heart aflame

And even though I know He'll love
Each one as much as me
That will never cause a problem
For in Heaven all agree

It's hard for us to contemplate
That Heavenly dwelling place
But the best will come when we get there
And meet Jesus face to face

He Rekindles The Flame

Our God above is a God of love
Which He daily pours out on His own
He longs to bless and even caress
Those open to the love He has shown

God gifts us with grace in the holy place
Where we gather to be centered on Him
When we're set apart just to bless His heart
He brightens each light that grows dim

He'll rekindle the flame for that is His aim
In His presence all that's vain fades away
As we rest in His love His pure Holy Dove
Enters in without any delay

Every second is sweet as we sit at His feet
And soak in His love and His peace
As we continue to soar toward The One we adore
All the storms in our lives seem to cease

Our hearts become full and we sense a pull
Deep within from the Spirit above
We have not a doubt it's time to reach out
To a world much in need of God's love

My Great Reward

There's a secret chamber in Your heart
Reserved for me alone
And I love to race to that heavenly place
Forsaking all that I own

For in that precious time dear Lord
That You use to shine on me
I'm at peace, unafraid, in the place that You've made
Where my soul is set free in Thee

It's so restful there without a care
In the shelter of the One up above
What a blessing to be completely set free
By the Son of the One that I love

In that special place with You dear Lord
I feel so light and free
So relaxed, refreshed and completely filled up
It hardly seems like me

I do not know why You bless me so
But this I do know Lord
I love You so and want all to know
That You are my great reward

Crowns To Lay At His Feet

Father I thank You a million times over
For the graces You've given to me
I'm blessed beyond measure with many a treasure
And each gives me the desire to be

All that would please my Heavenly Father
And bring much delight to His heart
For in your great plan there's room for each man
That You meant for him from the start

Every women and child has a place there as well
And we all have a job to complete
Each day if we will be sure to fulfill
We'll have crowns to lay at Your feet

What a joy it will be when we enter the Kingdom
And join the throngs that are there
Forever to love You to praise and adore You
Forever embraced in Your care

What A Time Of Rejoicing

My life I surrender to You Lord
For the purpose You see that I miss
I don't need to know, just be in the flow
For to live in Your will is pure bliss

Swing open the doors You want open
Close tightly the ones that remain
Let my life be so Yours, that my spirit life soars
Then all waste will be turned into gain

For my heart says it won't be too long
Till the Master comes back for His bride
He'll sweep up His own, take them home to His throne
And forever with them He'll abide

But before that should happen I pray
From the depths of my being within
Send revival oh God, send Your chastening rod
To flush out every stain of sin

Then all those who are presently lost
And dead in their desperate plight
With their blindness removed, they will thus be approved
Then blameless they'll be in Your sight

And for all those you've called on to pray
For the lost souls You love oh so much
What a time of rejoicing, the saints will be voicing
Their delight for the souls You did touch

His Fatherly Nod

The heavenly wings of the Father
Are spread around each child
Those born of the Spirit belong to Him
And shall not be defiled

In tenderness He teaches us
All that we need to know
So we will develop confidence
As we continue to learn and grow

Every test and trial that comes our way
Is filtered through the Father's hands
Because of His love, He fashions each one
So gently, cause He understands

How frail we are and in need of His grace
To help us overcome and be strong
And through each happenstance we pass
We are learning right from wrong

As we mature and grow up in the Lord
We become part of the army of God
And as we move out on the battlefield
He gives us His Fatherly nod

My Saviors Smile

Lord I plunge myself into that place
Where I'm all alone with You
And the sweetest communion I've ever known
Always comes shining through

Your gentle Presence sweeps over me
Like a blanket covering a child
What a lovely thought invades my mind
Upon me my Savior has smiled

Cozy and warm and close to You Lord
I rest in Your sweet caress
How pleasant it is to be filled with You
For You are my happiness

No wonder I rush to that meeting place
To chat with the One I adore
The love that I feel there is ever so real
And is always worth waiting for

Message Of Love

Oh let me be the container dear Lord
That holds Your dear Presence within
Teach me to give out what You've given to me
Aware that You will fill me again

For the treasure You pour into hearts that are open
Is not to be selfishly stored
But shared with many You see in Your vision
Who are hungry for more and are bored

The things of this world are weighing them down
And can bring no peace to their souls
Move mightily Lord and soften their hearts
As Your plan of salvation unfolds

All who adore You do want to be used
To carry Your message of love
It's a message that frees all those that are bound
And comes from the heart of our God up above

How much we need Your enabling Lord
For there's nothing we can do on our own
Fill us up to the fullest with all that we need
To sow the seeds that need to be sown

How I thank You for making it so dear Lord
That we can be part of Your plan
Filled with your joy, obeying Your word
As we carry Your message to man

A Clear Reflection

Melt my heart oh gentle Savor
Make me more like You each day
I long to be a clear reflection
Of your goodness Lord I pray

I give to you this earthen vessel
Do with me what're You please
Be it serving, giving, sharing
Or daily praying on my knees

I choose to be Your willing servant
Sensitive to what You say
Trusting You to lead and guide me
For I do not know the way

Only You know where you want me
What You would have me say and do
Help my heart to always listen
So that I'll be pleasing You

Those who hear and do Gods bidding
Sense a lasting joy inside
Way down deep within the temple
Where the Savior doth abide

His Ever Constant Aim

How inadequate we mortals feel
To reach our mighty God
That is until we learn how real
He is and that's not odd

Though often He seems far away
And our chances mighty slim
He's supplied us with a simple means
Of tuning in on Him

God can even hear the whisper
Of each child of His down here
Crying out in desperation
When overwhelmed by fear

However deep the sadness
However strong the pain
He has all it takes to free His own
And make them whole again

We need only seek His Presence
And call out His precious Name
For to love protect and bless us
Is His ever-constant aim

My Consecration

I search dear Lord within my soul
For words that can express
The depth of love I feel for You
The God I long to bless

There's so much stored within my heart
That wants to bubble out
And rise to reach You on Your throne
It makes me want to shout

But instead of letting it explode
In worship and in song
Sometimes I tend to hold it in
And this I know is wrong

Oh God remove the barriers
That so imprison me
And dam up all the love inside
I long to give to Thee

All the contents of my heart
I pour out before You now
This I do with reverence Lord
And in adoration bow

For nothing I give to You in love
Is ever a wasted gift
But a simple expression of my consecration
For You to weigh and sift

In His Presence

What a blessing it is to get quiet with You Lord
To reflect on all that You've made
Such beauty You've placed in this world You've created
Your wonders around us are richly displayed

Our hearts sing as we ponder the depths of Your love
That You daily pour out on Your own
Rich blessings overtake us as our praises ascend Lord
To bless You seated high on Your throne

Pour out Your Spirit so strongly upon us
That we miss nothing dear Lord You desire to give
Help us to respond to Your generous nature
For without Your fullness we shall not truly live

Draw us closer and closer to You in the stillness
For it's there that Your fullness brings tears to our eyes
It's there in Your Presence that we take on Your likeness
And all that offends You withers and dies

Your brightness takes over and wipes out the darkness
We take on the light of the Lord that we love
We shine with the love of our Heavenly Savior
God's spirit lives in us His sign is the dove

Happiness Is

Happiness is loving Jesus
Treasuring Him within my soul
Spending time in His dear Presence
Reflecting His goodness is my goal

Happiness is praising Jesus
Honoring Him in word and song
Singing of love of thanks and worship
My highest praises to Him belong

Happiness is being grateful
Thanking Jesus every day
Counting my blessings in His Presence
For He deserves a big hooray

Happiness is sharing Jesus
Telling others about His love
His merciful heart and His forgiveness
And His kingdom up above

Happiness is serving Jesus
Living in His perfect will
Being about His business daily
His dearest pleasures to fulfill

What a joy to know this Jesus
To carry Him always in my heart
To have Him as my dear companion
Never ever to depart

Miracles Happen

Thank You Dear Lord a million times over
For the grace You've extended to me
My hearts running over with multiple praises
And I fall on my face before Thee

Nothing is sweeter than the warmth of Your Presence
My heart delights to draw near
May the love that I bring and the thanks that I feel
Be to You a treasure most dear

As I bask in the Presence of the Lord I so cherish
And drink in the gift of His peace
With joyful expression I sing of His goodness
And pray that these moments increase

For the more that I offer my Heavenly Savior
The more blessing He heaps upon me
It's true as can be as the scriptures declare
He outshines in generosity

No one can linger for long in His Presence
Without change of some kind taking place
Miracles happen when we mingle with Jesus
And welcome His tender embrace

We Need Only Seek Deeper

Please open my eyes to see what You see
And to do what You'd have me to do
To learn to speak out what it's all about
For to You Lord I long to be true

To be one with You in the Spirit Lord
Is a desire close to my heart
To follow Your ways-to the end of my days
Is a longing only You could impart

There is a higher realm in the Spirit world
Those who are seeking are certain to find
Though available to all, there is only a small
Percentage of those with that mind

Who choose to seek deeper and push on beyond
That which they presently know
To the rewarding awareness of all of the fullness
Our God doth so long to bestow

What a shame it is some miss out on the wealth
That our Savior's so eager to give
We need only seek deeper from our Lord and keeper
To much more abundantly live

Our Sovereign God

Your mind is vast and extensive Lord
Far beyond what we understand
And that's the way You designed it to be
So we'll trust in Your plan, which is grand

You are a God who is sovereign and kind
All that You do is just right
As we yield to You and live in Your will
We'll then walk by faith not by sight

Our lives could flow so much easier Lord
If we would cease to be in control
Your blessings would flow like an avalanche
Much more quickly we'd reach our goal

For then we'd be led by Your Spirit
In all that we do and say
Spreading your message of truthfulness
As Your Spirit leaded the way

And that's what Your plan is all about
Extending Your love to the lost
Making great saints out of sinners
Regardless of what it might cost

A Pure Vessel

I treasure Your Presence dear God
More than anything else I hold dear
Your nearness within reveals any sin
That I need to deal with right here

Each day I want to be clean
A pure vessel through which You can flow
Wash over me, for this is my plea
And prepare me for where I must go

A fresh touch from You I must seek
This I will do each new day
Make my way clear, and help me to hear
I trust You to lead all the way

Only then can I truly give out
That which You've poured into me
Some will be blest, and welcome Your rest
And the praise will be given to Thee

His Caring Has No End

I long to bless-with a sweet caress
The Savior of my soul
One day near Him in my heavenly home
His Name I will extol

I pray my heart-will ne'r depart
From the One who died for me
He took my sins upon Himself
When He died on Calvary

He gave so much and His love was such
His caring has no end
All mankind He had in mind
Every heart He desires to mend

He wants none lost-whatever the cost
He seeks happiness for all
But sad to say-some will not obey
They refuse to heed His call

Let's pray-that they-will change one day
And open their hearts up wide
To receive the Savior of their souls
Forever in Him to abide

The Greatest Miracle

There's no one in this universe
More precious than the Lord
A million thanks and praises
In my heart for Him are stored

For He has shown Himself to be
A faithful loving friend
I'm sure He'll always be the same
Right up to the end

He's gentle and He has a way
Of mending broken hearts
And fixing shattered bodies
With His store of brand new parts

And in every situation
He has the best in view
There's not a single fractured life
He cannot make brand new

He reserves the greatest miracle
For those who long for more
Every lovely gift He has
Into their hearts He'll pour

A Foretaste Of Heaven

Be not dismayed if the plans you've made
Are not clearly laid out before you
For your Father above-has the plan of His love
And it's His plan He wants you to do

It's not from your mind that this plan is designed
But comes straight from the heart of God
His wisdom is such-and He loves us so much
That sometimes He must use the rod

He wants us on track-away from the pack
So we can hear with a listening ear
Then we act on the facts that He's given to us
And this we can do without fear

For His mind is divine-and one of a kind
Surely we can depend upon Him
To impart His light both day and night
As He fills us full up to the brim

He wants us to seek-then get a clear peek
With the spiritual eye that He's given
It's then that the child of the Father we love
Gets a wonderful foretaste of heaven

God's Kingdom Is Near

O Light of the world shine brightly on me
Blast through the darkness and help me to see
Enlighten my mind with Your filtering rays
So I may see clearly the rest of my days

The gift of discernment I seek from You Lord
Not to be selfish, for I don't want to hoard
But to use it wisely as all gifts should be used
For no gift You give should e'er be abused

Please distribute this gift Lord not just to me
But to all who are Yours that all may perceive
The vision You've given to each of Your own
Then fruit will come forth from the seeds that are sown

Lord it's then that Your will can be brought into being
For each of Your own will truly be seeing
Through the eyes of The Spirit, we all hold so dear
We do hunger to serve you, Your Kingdoms so near

Blessings

How can I ever thank You Lord
For blessings small and great
Each one designed with love by You
And they are never late

Blessings come in many forms
Right from Your caring heart
And it delights You thoroughly
Your treasures to impart

Each one is extra special
Meant to touch my soul
And each one an encouragement
To help me reach my goal

Which is to go on serving You
In any way You choose
For as long as I am able Lord
My time is Yours to use

And when my life draws to a close
I'll listen for Your voice
Calling me into Your Kingdom
Where forever I'll rejoice

A Safe Anchor

You are our shepherd Lord
We are Your sheep
You promised Your comfort
At times when we'd weep

Wrap us in the shelter
Of Your loving embrace
As we encounter the trials
That we all must face

You are a safe anchor
In the storms of life
We can count on Your Presence
In the midst of our strife

You extend Your sweet graces
You fill us with peace
And to all who are Yours
Your dear blessings increase

We rest in Your arms Lord
Our strength and our song
And give You our hearts
For to You we belong

Ode To My King

My joy is ever praising You
My Lord-my God-my King
As I ponder on all You are to me
It makes me want to sing

Alleluias and hosannas
To the One who feeds my soul
As long as I have breath in me
I'll never change my goal

I'll spend my days in happy praise
Then I'll send it on to You
With all the love my heart contains
For I cherish the God I pursue

You are my song-my tower of strength
My refuge-my hiding place
I love to nestle under Your wings
Where You daily pour out Your grace

There is no other place of comfort
Like that which Your Presence brings
Your treasures I would never trade
For the wealth of ten thousand kings

A Special Joy

When Gods' people get together to worship their Creator
Explosive things begin to happen in that place
Jesus joins the gathering, love is everywhere
And the Spirit of God spreads peace on every face

Our praises fill the atmosphere-the Holy Spirit's present
And the sweetness of the Lord is oh so real
His joy invades His people melting every blockage
And even broken hearts begin to heal

The children of the King get lost in adoration
And tears begin to flow from lowered eyes
Hearts begin to soften, forgiveness freely flows
And those who need uniting make new ties

No wonder there's an eagerness to assemble all together
With the members of His church in one accord
Worship that's astounding-happiness abounding
What a special joy this must be to the Lord

To You Lord I'll Cling

How I thank you dear Lord
I have access to You
It's because of Your grace
That You pour out anew

You've made Yourself known
In the sweetest of ways
Oh I praise and I thank You
For you light up my days

You sweep into my heart
At the break of each dawn
And gladden my moments
Till the day is all gone

Your love warms and refreshes
Your peace settles in
And I feel such contentment
On my face there's a grin

What a glorious gift
Is the joy that You bring
For the rest of my days
To You Lord I'll cling

Life More Abundantly

I love You Lord with all my heart
And never tire of telling You so
You are the Creator of everything
The heavens and all that's below

As I rest by Your grace, in Your precious peace
And ponder the mysteries of old
Each one points to You in all of Your glory
If the pure truth should ever be told

For who can compare to Your awesomeness
Or to the majestic works of Your hand
For all are displayed magnificently
As we travel throughout this great land

From the oceans deep to the mountains high
And to all else that our eyes can perceive
It all came about from the words that You spoke
Though that is hard for some to believe

You in Your greatness hold it all in place
And govern like the King that You are
Oh mighty and glorious God of us all
You shine brighter than any star

Light up our lives and shine through us Lord
That all will awaken and see
The joy that comes to the one who receives
That life more abundantly

Jesus What A Beautiful Name

Jesus what a beautiful name
To me like a lovely refrain
At times that Name brings tears to my eyes
When I think how His loss was my gain

I whisper His Name in the night
When it's peaceful without any light
And I recall how special He's been to me
As I cling to His Word oh so tight

There's power in our dear Saviors name
Sufficient to break every chain
Those who are bound find freedom in Him
And one day will enter His reign

What a day of sweet joy that will be
For in Heaven we'll all be set free
From the trials and burdens of this present life
Oh what glorious sights we shall see

God's Generous Endowment

What an abundant giver our God is
We are surrounded by beauty and love
We oft take for granted His generous endowment
Neglecting to give thanks to our God up above

Time is a gift He has given His children
It's meant to be used with great care
For hours each day slip through our fingers
We must all set aside more time to share

For the good news of Jesus has been given to us
What a blessing we Christians possess
What is given to us must be given to others
If we are to complete the process

There are souls who have never heard of the Savior
And they need to receive and be saved
Let's heed the call and share Jesus with them
That in God's book their names be engraved

What a joy it will be to one day see those
That received God's dear message from us
Sharing the blessed wonders of heaven
All because in God's word they did trust

Eternal Dream

Wake up Your body that's sleeping oh Lord
By Your penetrating gaze
Cause us to stand up and be counted
Shake us out of this haze

For what have You got to work with
If Your saints don't surrender to You
The work won't get done that was left by Your Son
So what is there left to do?

O God helps us to catch Your vision
And get on with the work that remains
Please give us Your wisdom and insight
And invigorate our brains

We need to be united with You Lord
We need to work as a team
The Head and the body together
To fulfill Your eternal dream

With Jesus We Have It All

I'm one with the Lord and have fun with the Lord
He's not a stuffed shirt you know
He's gentle and loving-not prone to shoving
His children as they flourish and grow

He treats each with kindness never with blindness
His smile daily lights up the sky
No wonder His children love to be near Him
With Jesus you really fly high

Whatever comes your way on any given day
He's there waiting to help you out
Just give Him a chance your life He'll enhance
For that's what He's all about

Take a tip from me-check it out and see
If what I'm saying isn't right on the ball
There is nothing to lose but so much to gain
For with Jesus we have it all

Thoughts Of Christmas

What Christmas Is To Me

Christmas to me was a year-end thing
For many and many a season
The truth of Christmas evaded me
I knew not what the reason

Much of the year there was pain and trials
And then at Christmas time
Everyone bubbled and sparkled
And everything seemed to be fine

But then the Christmas lights were removed
And the tree was thrown away
And the ornaments were boxed up again
To take out another day

It seemed to me that the Christmas joy
And the smiles on the faces of many
Got boxed away with the ornaments
To me this seemed uncanny

Then one special day Jesus entered my life
And changed my darkness to light
And since then Christmas lives in my heart
And each day is ever so bright

Not that there's never a trial to face
But my God watches over me
And brings forth good from every one
He's a faithful God you see

He's able to do remarkable things
In each life surrendered to Him
How delighted I am He's entered my heart
And filled me right up to the brim

A Reason To Celebrate

Jesus' birthday's drawing near
What a time for joy
As we celebrate the coming
Of God the Father's Baby Boy

His entrance changed the whole wide world
For all eternity
And a way was made for each of us
To live a life that's free

Free from chronic sin and evil
That permeates this earth
And that's a special reason
To celebrate Christ's birth

But there's an even greater reason
That I'm glad to share with you
All who give their hearts to Jesus
And are truly born anew

Will reign with Christ forever
In never ending bliss
And it's Jesus precious love for us
We have to thank for this

Christmas To Me

Christmas to me is not just a tree
All covered with silver and gold
Nor a jolly old elf driving by himself
Through the sky on a night so cold

Its not special sites all twinkling with lights
Nor packages wrapped to a T
While all this is nice it will not suffice
If the Source of our lives we'll not see

These traditions are fun but keep us on the run
As we rush to squeeze everything in
So all will be right on Christmas Eve night
And the celebration then can begin

We get so involved we forget to resolve
Any differences we may have with our kin
How can we believe we will truly receive
The Christ Child within if there's sin

We must keep our hearts clean so that we may glean
From the One who created us all
Blessings astounding and graces abounding
Only then can we answer His call

Christmas you see is Christ in you and me
Each and every new day
It's not what we do but Christ flowing through
As we listen to Him and obey

Christmas to me is being set free
By The Savior The Light of our lives
My prayer is steady that we'll all be ready
Whenever His Kingdom arrives

The True Christmas Story

The true Christmas story never gets stale
Cause it is absolute truth not a fairy tale
Long, long ago God devised a plan
To send His Son to become a man

So Jesus came down from Heaven to earth
And His truly was a miracle birth
Born of a virgin in a stable that day
He was tenderly wrapped and laid in the hay

The oxen and sheep and calves kept Him warm
From the dampness of night or a threatening storm
Mary and Joseph looked on with delight
As shepherds came to witness this holy sight

While they worshipped baby Jesus angels sang from on high
And a beautiful star lit up the night sky
This star led the wise men who came to adore
After traveling far with their gifts galore

The heavens rang with the sound of the angel's song
Can't you just picture that awesome throng?
Time elapsed and Jesus grew in stature and grace
Till the time for Him came to enter that place

Of walking each day in His Father's will
Always first in His mind Father's will to fulfill
Finally it led Him to His death on the cross
His precious life was snuffed out but all was not loss

For His death meant the canceling of all of our sin
If we will receive His great gift and begin again
Dear God thank You for the sweet gift of love Jesus brought
Please help us to live each day, as we ought

A Holy Christmas

Christmas time is near once more
Excitement fills the air
Shoppers rushing to and fro
Selecting gifts with care

Families busy with many things
In preparation of
That special day that's not far off
When each one spreads his love

With all the busyness there is
Writing cards and such
Baking, shopping, seeing friends
Doing way to much

How often do we take the time
To quiet down and be
In the presence of the Lord
Who came for you and me?

Refreshing ourselves as we wait on Him
Basking in His precious love
Giving thanks for His mercy and grace
That flows from the heavens above

Wouldn't we then be much more at ease
When that special day finally arrives
And more able to spread His love in us
To our own and others besides

Dearest Jesus we thank You for coming to earth
And Lord we just want to say
We love You and praise You and give our lives
To You on Your birthday

Thank You Dear Lord For Christmas

Thank You dear Lord for Christmas
What a lovely time of year
Hearts are light and spirits bright
It's a time to spread good cheer

All around are twinkling lights
And happy smiling faces
Little ones are all aglow
It seems to touch all races

Christmas is a busy time
With so much preparation
Please help us Lord to not lose sight
Of this meaningful celebration

For long ago - 2000 years
You left Your Fathers throne
And came to earth to make a way
For sinners to "come home"

You gave Your life to set men free
From the sin that plagues mankind
Willing were You to shed Your blood
To open the eyes of the blind

Please open the hearts that are empty Lord
To receive the gift of Your love
So that many who now live in darkness
Will this Christmas "be born from above"

Christmas

C is for the Christ Child born in Bethlehem
H is for the Heavens where dwell the cherubim
R is the Roughness of the hay in Jesus bed
I is for the Inn from which the Holy Family fled
S is for the Simple Way our Savior came to earth
T is for the Time God chose for Jesus holy birth
M is for Christ's Mother who surrendered to God's will
A is for the Angels, their song the air did fill
S is for the Shiny Star that blazed up in the sky
Awakening the shepherds and now also you and I

Jesus came that day so long ago
And lived a sinless life
He died a cruel and painful death
To free us from such strife

We need to heed the message
That Jesus came to give
And open up our hearts to Him
Where He so longs to live

Our hearts will then be joyful
As we live to please our King
Regardless of the cost to us
For we owe Him everything

Christmas Love

Each year in late December
Comes a season of Christmas love
When we recall that our heavenly Father
Sent His Son from His home up above

The wonder of God's indescribable Gift
Came to earth in baby form
He was laid in a bed of straw that night
With sheep near to keep Him warm

Christ willingly came to open the gates
That were closed by Adam's sin
He suffered and died for the sake of us all
Oh - let's open our hearts to Him

His coming was also to teach us
To follow His pattern for living
So we in turn could surrender our lives
To bless others by our loving and giving

There's never been one like Jesus
And never again will there be
His precious presence in our lives
Is a treasure for you and for me

So let's live each day in this Christmas love
That Jesus so lovingly gives
Lifting our love and our thanks to Him
For it's deep in our hearts that He lives

My Christmas Prayer

Thoughts of Jesus - oh - so tiny
In a manger come to me
As we ready ourselves for Christmas
And prepare to trim the tree

How often do we deeply ponder
The depth of Jesus' sacrifice
As He left His home in Heaven
To come to earth to give His life

What an awesome gift God's given
To all whose hearts will open wide
His own dear Son - so pure - so holy
Desires most eagerly to reside inside

And when He enters a heart that's hungry
He brings with Him His holy love
His joy to fill the empty places
And His peace descending like a dove

We who deeply - truly love Him
At this time of year rejoice
That He's spoken clearly to us
And that we have heard His voice

There are multitudes that shun Him
And reject His gift so rare
Oh - that their hearts will open to Him
Is my fervent Christmas prayer

The Miracle Of Christmas

Long ago, two thousand years
A grand event took place
The Holy Son of God came down
And joined the human race

He choose to take on human flesh
And do His Fathers will
To teach us how to live on earth
God's pleasure to fulfill

His life was spent in doing good
And helping those in need
He healed the sick and raised the dead
And multitudes did feed

The miracles He did perform
The Bible does make plain
All things He did were out of love
And not for selfish gain

And when His life on earth was up
They nailed Him to a tree
Crucified, for us He died
From sin He set us free

Our part is reaching out to Him
Receiving our salvation
Welcoming Him into our hearts
The King of all creation

We recall at Christmas time
The birth of Christ our Lord
A time when Jesus is to be
Both worshiped and adored

So let's prepare our hearts to sing
And celebrate His birth
Let's thank Him for His choice to come
And live down here on earth

Season Of Love

That wonderful season of Christmas
Draws near to us once again
When the Spirit of love comes upon us
Invading the hearts of men

There's a lovely feeling of warmness
Filling the atmosphere
And a sense of awe as we ponder
What makes special this time of year?

It's the birth of our Savior, the Christ Child
We are preparing to celebrate
Our thoughts carry us back to the manger
On which we meditate

We think of the very Son of God
Leaving His home high above
To enter the world for the sake of us all
To draw us back to Himself through His love

He willingly suffered and died for each one
That accepting His gift we might gain
Eternal bliss in His Kingdom
Where upon His throne He will reign

One day this life will be over
But there is a richer one by far
For those who love and accept Him
And those who do, know who they are

Christmas Musings

Have you ever pondered the sweet sounds from Heaven
Announcing to the world Christ's birth?
As the angels sang out with grand voices of joy
Excitement must have covered the earth

Can you just imagine the heart of Christ's mother
Overflowing with gratefulness and love?
For the honor to be chosen to carry within her
The Messiah-Gods sweet gift from above

And have you considered Gods special blessing
To the shepherds that first Christmas night?
The glorious privilege to gaze on the Savior
Can you picture what an awesome sight

What would you have given to be led as the wise men
By the brilliance of the Christmas star?
How brightly it twinkled and shone in the night
Leading them onward as they came from afar

Even the animals that attended sweet Jesus
We're chosen by God to be near
The tender scene that unfolded that first Christmas night
Is re-enacted again each new year

Which brings us once more to that time fast approaching
So precious to each generation
For Christmas is coming and soon will be here
And its time for a fresh consecration

So open your heart afresh to the Savior
Turn your life over to Him
Allow Him to shine through that vessel you live in
Instead of the tree- your heart trim

Christmas Star

Bright and gleaming Christmas star
Shining up above
Guide us to the Christ Child's crib
Where we can sense His love

Send your glow down here below
And by your dazzling light
Our eyes will glimpse the wonder of
That very first Christmas night

Illuminate within our hearts
That spark that's hidden deep
So it will burst into a flame
That only God can keep

With spirit eyes we'll visualize
The manger scene once more
And with increasing reverence
We'll bow down and adore

Our loving Savior longs to bless
His children here below
With grand and glorious treasures
We can't begin to know

As we receive His peace and joy
We'll spread it all around
And to every heart that's open
His blessings will abound

Oh Christmas star do lead the way
As you did so long ago
And as we celebrate Christ's birth
Our hearts will overflow

Treasuring Christmas

Christmas is a joyful time
We all look forward to
Though we wish we could eradicate
Some things there are to do

Shopping, baking, wrapping
And trimming up the tree
Writing out the Christmas cards
These all take time you see

It could be so much easier
If we would just slow down
Close our tired weary eyes
And blot out every sound

Then think of all our blessings
And the love God has for us
How much He wants to help us
If we would only trust

Let's take some time to give Him thanks
And rest in His sweet peace
Receive the blessings of His love
And feel our tensions cease

If the Holy Son of God most high
Had not come to live on earth
And give His life for all of us
We could not celebrate His birth

This means there'd be no Christmas
Our favorite time of year
That's floods our souls with joys untold
And memories so dear

It's time to treasure Christmas
As the birthday of our King
Crucified - for us He died
We owe Jesus everything

Christmas Questionnaire

When birthdays come we select with care
A very special gift
To delight the heart of someone
And gives that one a lift

Christmas is Christ's birthday
Do we follow suit and bring
The best we have to offer
To our Savior and our King

Do we set aside the time we need
To be alone with Him
To get to know our dearest Friend
So our lights do not grow dim

Do we linger in His presence
A little longer every day
To receive from Him the grace we need
To help us on our way

Do we recognize the many gifts
He gives to those who choose
To love Him much and put Him first
And always seek His views

Do we make it a priority
To daily read His holy Word
To meditate upon it
And share what we just heard

And how much time is set apart
To enter into prayer
To ask His intervention
In the lives of those we share

With all that Jesus does for us
And has done in the past
Let's love Him much and bless His heart
With treasures that will last

Our Christmas Focus

Dearest Jesus we want to be focused on You
Not only on Christmas but all the year through
For You are our Savior our Shepherd and Friend
Who promised to be with us to the very end

All during the year You come through for us Lord
When we are discouraged worn out or bored
We know where to turn to receive what we need
You are eager to help us we don't have to plead

You lovingly care for Your children down here
From Your multiple blessings You make that so clear
We humbly welcome Your peace and Your love
Pure treasures from heaven coming down from above

As Your birthday approaches our gifts we do bring
To cherish and honor our Savior and King
So loved are You Lord our hearts overflow
Please grant us the grace to shine with Your glow

LaVergne, TN USA
05 December 2010

207521LV00001B/175/P

9 781452 070278